I0814937

Music Superstars
OLIVIA RODRIGO
TORQUE
BY SUZANE NGUYEN
BELLWETHER MEDIA · MINNEAPOLIS, MN

Torque brims with excitement perfect for thrill-seekers of all kinds. Discover daring survival skills, explore uncharted worlds, and marvel at mighty engines and extreme sports. In *Torque* books, anything can happen. Are you ready?

This edition first published in 2025 by Bellwether Media, Inc.

Library of Congress Cataloging-in-Publication Data

Names: Nguyen, Suzane, author.
Title: Olivia Rodrigo / by Suzane Nguyen.
Description: Minneapolis, MN : Bellwether Media, 2025. | Series: Music superstars | Includes bibliographical references and index. | Audience: Ages 7-12 | Audience: Grades 4-6 | Summary: "Engaging images accompany information about Olivia Rodrigo. The combination of high-interest subject matter and light text is intended for students in grades 3 through 7"– Provided by publisher.
Identifiers: LCCN 2024047012 (print) | LCCN 2024047013 (ebook) | ISBN 9798893042665 (library binding) | ISBN 9798893043631 (ebook)
Subjects: LCSH: Rodrigo, Olivia–Juvenile literature. | Singers–United States–Biography–Juvenile literature. | Actors–United States–Biography–Juvenile literature. | LCGFT: Biographies.
Classification: LCC ML3930.R634 N48 2025 (print) | LCC ML3930.R634 (ebook) | DDC 782.42164092 [B]–dc23/eng/20241008
LC record available at https://lccn.loc.gov/2024047012
LC ebook record available at https://lccn.loc.gov/2024047013

Editor: Rachael Barnes Designer: Josh Brink

Printed in the United States of America, North Mankato, MN.

TABLE OF CONTENTS

A PERFORMANCE TO REMEMBER

Olivia Rodrigo takes the stage at the 2024 **Grammy Awards**. Piano notes quietly open her song “vampire.” A spotlight shines on Olivia as she sings.

BEST DRESSED

Olivia enjoys bringing new life to old looks. She often wears clothes from the 1990s and 2000s.

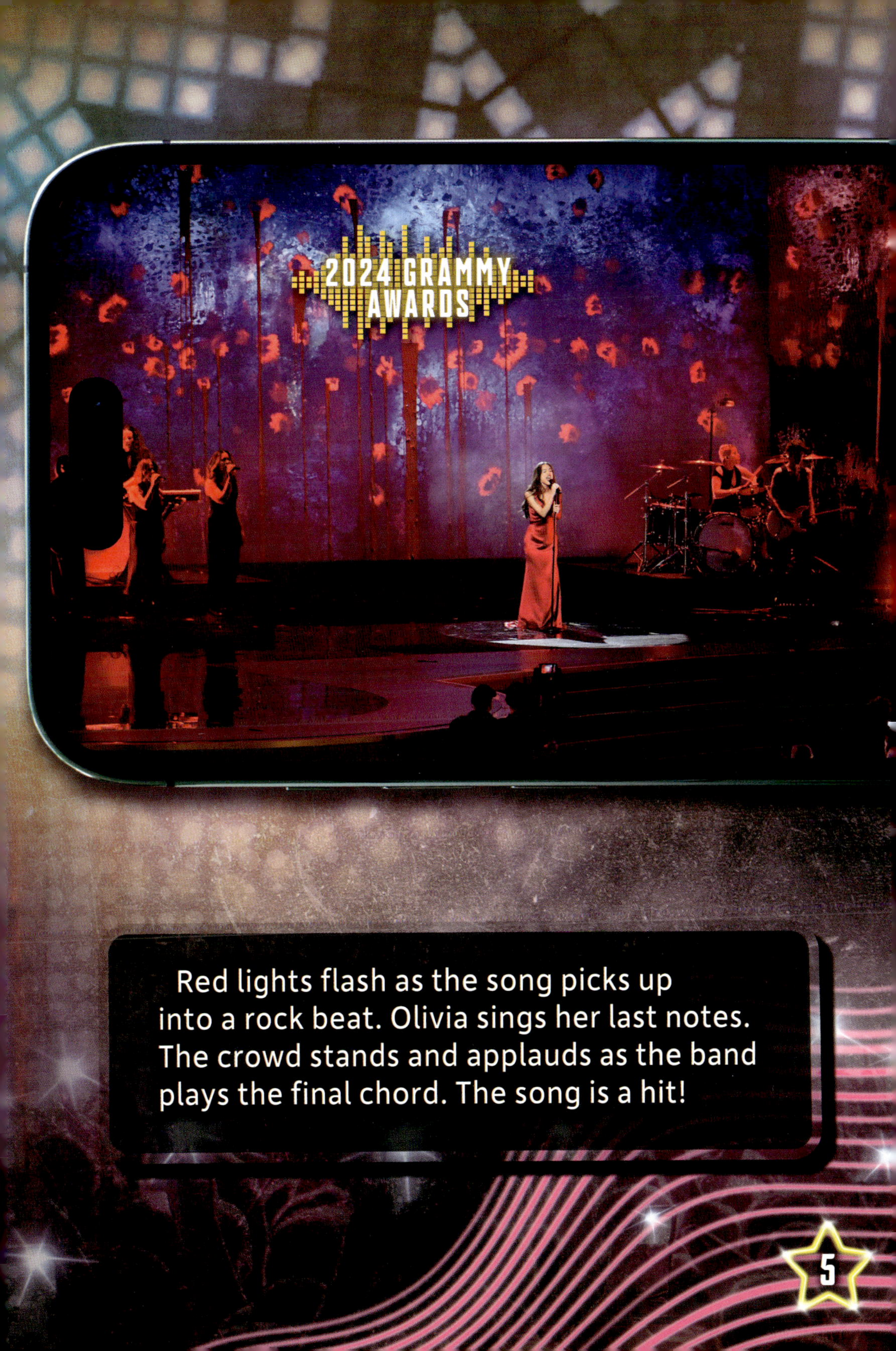

Red lights flash as the song picks up into a rock beat. Olivia sings her last notes. The crowd stands and applauds as the band plays the final chord. The song is a hit!

WHO IS OLIVIA RODRIGO?

Olivia Rodrigo is a pop singer. She first gained fame as an actress. Since her **solo** music career began in 2021, she has won many music awards.

OLIVIA RODRIGO

Birthday	Hometown	Type of Music	First Solo Hit
February 20, 2003	Murrieta, California	pop	"drivers license"

Olivia supports many **charities**. She started her own charity to support the education and safety of young women. She also gives money to shelters that help women.

GETTING INTO PERFORMING

Olivia got into music when she was young. Her mom introduced her to rock music. When she was 5, she began singing lessons. Olivia started acting lessons at age 6.

MODELING SUPERSTAR

In 2010, Olivia modeled for an Old Navy commercial!

Olivia was 9 years old when she learned to play the piano. The lessons helped her as she began writing her own songs.

In 2015, Olivia starred in an American Girl movie called *Grace Stirs Up Success*. This was her first acting role. She was only 12 years old!

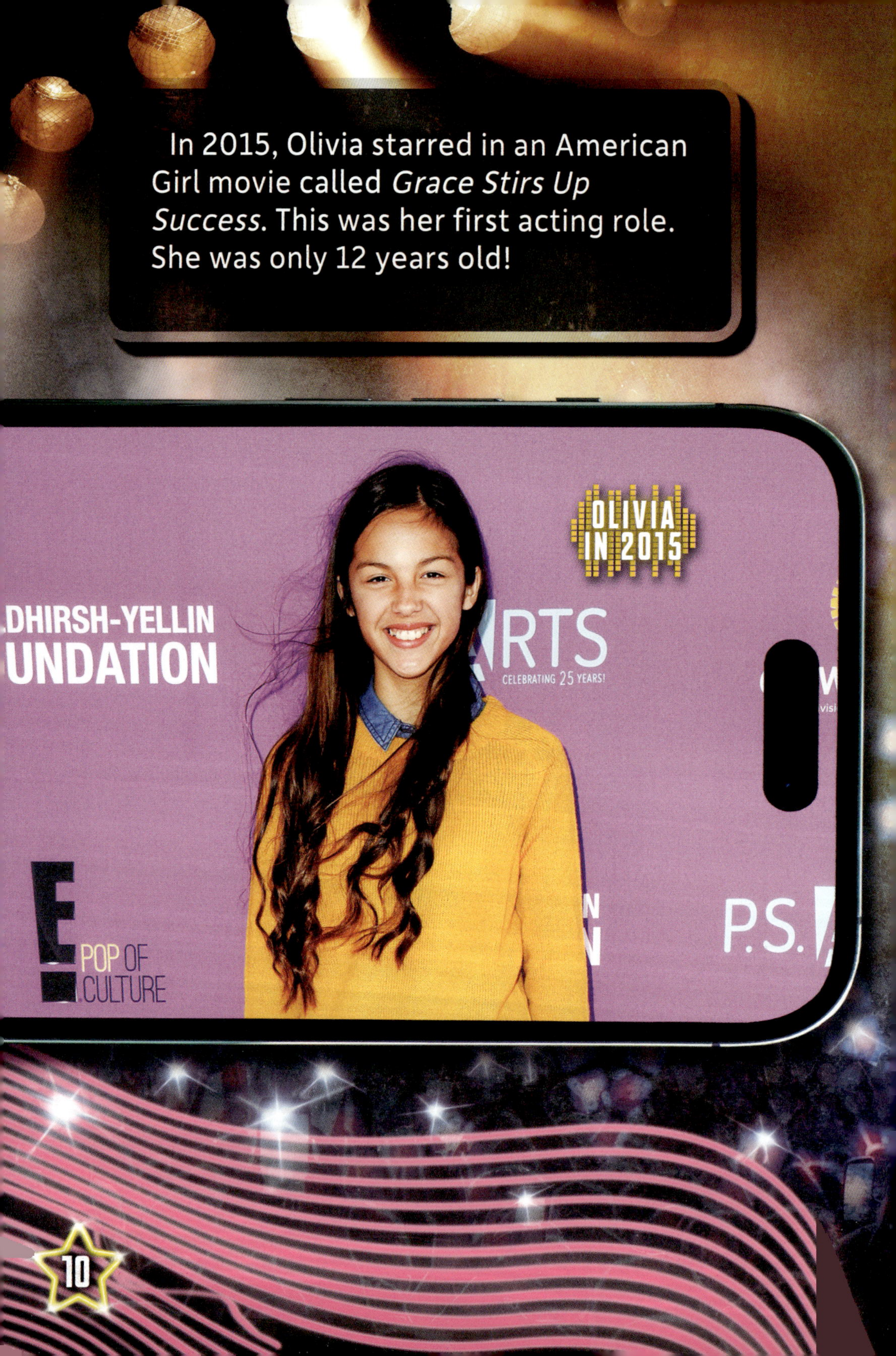

Starting in 2016, Olivia starred as one of the leads for the Disney Channel show *Bizaardvark*. She learned to play guitar for the show.

FROM ACTOR TO SINGER

In 2019, Olivia began working on a new Disney Channel show. She played Nini in *High School Musical: The Musical: The Series.*

TIMELINE

– 2016 –

Olivia begins acting as a lead in Disney Channel's *Bizaardvark*

– 2019 –

Olivia stars in Disney Channel's *High School Musical: The Musical: The Series*

Olivia was only 16 years old when she wrote and performed an original song for the show. "All I Want" quickly became a fan favorite! The song's success helped her sign with a **record label** in 2020.

– 2021 –

Olivia releases her first single, "drivers license"

– 2022 –

Olivia wins three Grammys, two for her album *SOUR*, and one for her song "drivers license"

– 2023 –

Olivia releases her second album, *GUTS*

In 2021, Olivia **released** her first single, "drivers license." It **debuted** at number one on the ***Billboard*** Hot 100 chart. The song was there for eight weeks! It became 2021's most **streamed** song on **Spotify**.

2022 PERFORMANCE OF "DRIVERS LICENSE"

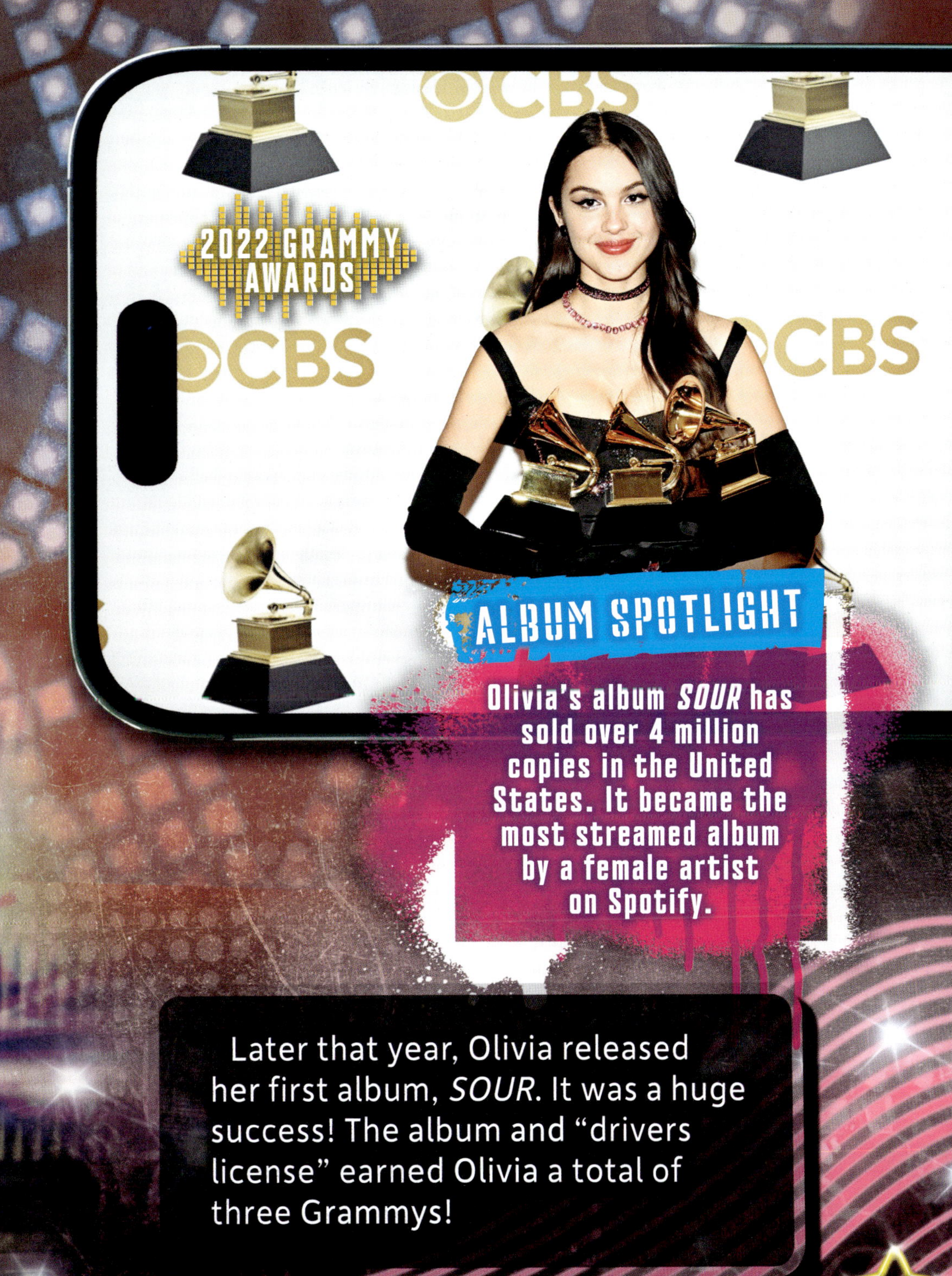

ALBUM SPOTLIGHT

Olivia's album *SOUR* has sold over 4 million copies in the United States. It became the most streamed album by a female artist on Spotify.

Later that year, Olivia released her first album, *SOUR*. It was a huge success! The album and "drivers license" earned Olivia a total of three Grammys!

In 2022, Olivia took a break from acting to focus on her music. In 2023, Olivia released a new song called “vampire.” The song was a huge hit! She became the first artist to have the lead singles from two albums in a row debut at number one!

That September, Olivia released her second album. *GUTS* debuted at number one, too!

AWARDS

as of October 2024

3 Grammy Awards

4 People's Choice Awards

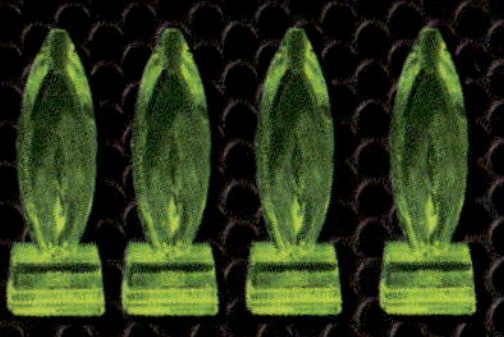

7 *Billboard* Music Awards

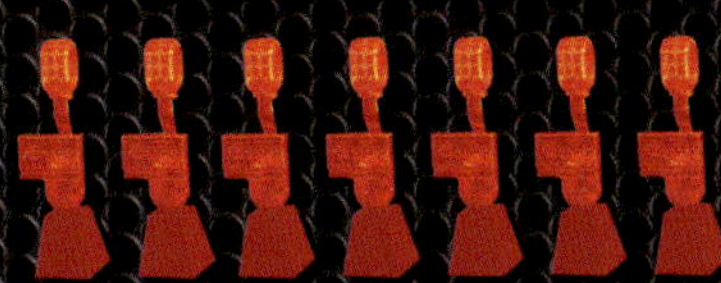

1 American Music Award

2023 MTV VIDEO MUSIC AWARDS

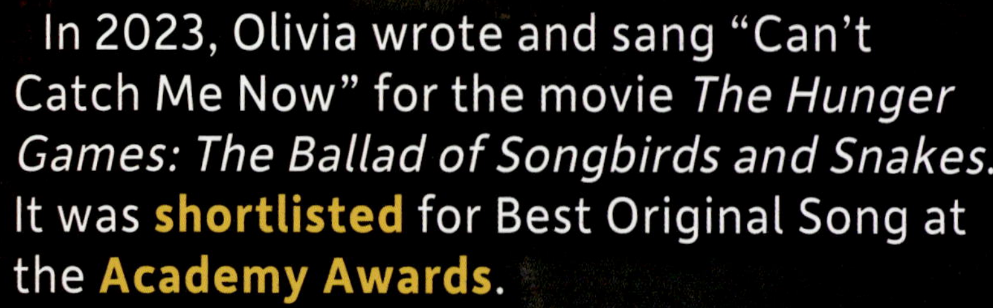

In 2023, Olivia wrote and sang “Can’t Catch Me Now” for the movie *The Hunger Games: The Ballad of Songbirds and Snakes*. It was **shortlisted** for Best Original Song at the **Academy Awards**.

Olivia kicked off her GUTS tour in 2024. She used her charity, Fund 4 Good, to give money from some of her ticket sales to charities in different countries.

FOR THE FANS

Olivia Rodrigo's fans are called Livies. They often dress up in late 1990s and early 2000s fashion for her concerts. Many wear black boots, skirts, and jean jackets.

FROM BAD TO GOOD

Olivia writes many songs. She says many are bad. But she believes the process helps her write the good ones.

PLAYLIST

"Driver's License" (2021)

"Deja Vu" (2021)

"Vampire" (2023)

"Bad Idea Right?" (2023)

"Can't Catch Me Now" (2023)

Livies find Olivia's music **relatable** and full of emotion. She often sings about heartbreak. Olivia continues to **inspire** many young fans!

GLOSSARY

Academy Awards—yearly awards presented for achievements in film; Academy Awards are also called Oscars.

Billboard—related to a well-known music news magazine and website that ranks songs and albums

charities—organizations that help others in need

debuted—was introduced or released for the first time

Grammy Awards—yearly awards given by the Recording Academy of the United States for achievements in music; Grammy Awards are also called Grammys.

inspire—to give someone an idea about what to do or create

record label—a company that sells music

relatable—able to be understood and connected to another person's experiences

released—made music available for listening

shortlisted—selected from a larger group being considered for an award

solo—relating to music performed by one person

Spotify—a streaming service that allows people to listen to music, podcasts, and audiobooks

streamed—listened to or played online

TO LEARN MORE

AT THE LIBRARY

Allen, Nafeesah. *What You Never Knew About Olivia Rodrigo.* North Mankato, Minn.: Capstone Press, 2023.

Gottlieb, Beth. *Olivia Rodrigo.* Buffalo, N.Y.: Enslow Publishing, 2024.

Rose, Rachel. *Olivia Rodrigo: Actor and Singer.* Minneapolis, Minn.: Bearport Publishing, 2023.

ON THE WEB

FACTSURFER

Factsurfer.com gives you a safe, fun way to find more information.

1. Go to www.factsurfer.com.
2. Enter "Olivia Rodrigo" into the search box and click 🔍.
3. Select your book cover to see a list of related content.

INDEX

The images in this book are reproduced through the courtesy of: Efren Landaos/ Sipa USA/ AP Newsroom, front cover (Olivia Rodrigo); Catsense, front cover (lights); Taya Ovod, pp. 2-3; MediaPunch Inc/ Alamy, pp. 3, 7; Kevin Winter/ Getty Images, p. 4; JC Olivera/ WireImage/ Getty Images, p. 5; Jordan Strauss/ Invision/ AP Newsroom, p. 6; Christopher Polk/ Billboard/ Getty Images, pp. 7 (infographic), 21; Nicole Wilder/ ©Disney Channel/ Everett Collection, pp. 8-9; Isaac Brekken Stringer/ Getty Images, p. 9; Richard Shotwell/ Invision/ AP Newsroom, p. 10; Craig Sjodin/ ©Disney Channel/ Everett Collection, p. 11; Film Fan/ Wikipedia, p. 11 (*La La Land*); Elena11, p. 11 (paint swatch); Tinseltown, p. 11 (Taylor Swift); ND700, p. 11 (ice skates); Jenny Anderson/ Getty Images, pp. 12-13; Disney Channel/ Wikipedia, p. 12 (*High School Musical: The Musical: The Series*); Rangel's Version/ Wikipedia, pp. 13 (*SOUR*), 21 (*SOUR*); (49 KB) Lk95/ Wikipedia, pp. 13 (*GUTS*), 21 (*GUTS*); Dabarti CGI, pp. 12-13 (timeline mixing board); Chris Polk/ Variety/ Penske Media/ Getty Images, p. 14; Brian Friedman/ Variety/ Penske Media/ Getty Images, p. 15; Jorge Estrellado/ TheNEWS2/ Alamy, p. 16; Charles Sykes/ Invision/ AP Newsroom, p. 17; CarlosVdeHabsburgo/ Wikipedia, p. 17 (Grammy Awards); Kathy Hutchins, p. 17 (*Billboard* Music Awards); s_bukley, p. 17 (People's Choice Awards, American Music Awards); Frazer Harrison/ Getty images, p. 18; Kevin Mazur/ Getty Images, p. 19; Everett Collection Inc/ Alamy, p. 20; jbrink, p. 21 ("Can't Catch Me Now" album); Justin Higuchi/ Wikipedia, p. 23.